2165

Putt and Play

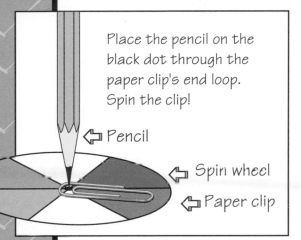

Place the pencil on the black dot through the paper clip's end loop. Spin the clip!

⇦ Pencil

⇦ Spin wheel

⇦ Paper clip

The Number of Players: 2–4

The Object of the Game: To complete each of the five holes on the miniature golf course in the fewest number of spins.

The Playing Pieces: A different type of marker for each player, such as a coin or a button; paper and pencil; and a paper clip.

The Play: The first player places his or her marker on the starting tee on hole #1. He or she spins the spinner, moves to the matching color area, and makes a tally mark to represent that spin (see **Scoring**). The player continues until the spinner lands on white. He or she then completes the hole by moving his or her marker to the white "cup." If the spinner hasn't landed on white after 4 spins, the player automatically moves to white. Each of the other players then plays hole #1. When all the players have completed that hole, they move to the next hole. A hazard or bonus on each hole may add to or subtract from a player's score.

Scoring: Each player records each spin on a piece of paper by making a tally mark with a pencil. A tally mark for 1 spin would look like this: I. Tally marks for 3 spins would look like this: III. For the fifth spin, a slash is drawn across 4 tally marks: ℍℍ. Tally marks for 9 spins would look like this: ℍℍ IIII.

The Winner: The player with the lowest score wins the game.

Math Concepts: Tallying. Adding by counting on. Counting by 5's.

PLAY BALL

SPORTS MATH

TIME
LIFE for
Children

ALEXANDRIA, VIRGINIA

ALL ABOUT
I LOVE MATH

Watch me throw the shot and solve some tricky riddles on page 60.

Dear Parent,

The *I Love Math* series shows children that math is all around them in everything they do. It can be found at the grocery store, at a soccer game, in the kitchen, at the zoo, even in their own bodies. As you collect this series, each book will fill in another piece of your child's world, showing how math is a natural part of everyday activities.

What Is Math?

Math is much more than manipulating numbers; the goal of math education today is to help children become problem solvers. This means teaching kids to observe the world around them by looking for patterns and relationships, estimating, measuring, comparing, and using reasoning skills. From an early age, children do this naturally. They divide up cookies to share with friends, recognize shapes in pizza, measure how tall they have grown, or match colors and patterns as they dress themselves. Young children love math. But when math only takes the form of abstract formulas on worksheets, children begin to dislike it. The *I Love Math* series is designed to keep math natural and appealing.

Help the ladybug team figure out the dot patterns on page 51!

How Do Children Learn Math?

Research has shown that children learn best by doing. Therefore, *I Love Math* is a hands-on, interactive learning experience. The math concepts are woven into stories in which entertaining characters invite your child to help them solve math challenges. Activities reinforce the concepts, and parent notes offer ways you and your child can have more fun with this program.

We have worked closely with math educators to include in these books a full range of math skills. As the series progresses, repetition of these skills in different formats will help your child master the basics of mathematical thinking.

What Will You Find in *Sports Math*?

In *Sports Math* you will quickly discover that math and sports go hand in hand. Your child will add up inning scores at a baseball game; measure distances around a track; compare the heights and jumps of slam-dunking basketball players; predict the winner of a swimming race; and use a soccer ball to learn about probability. Bowling, archery, and golf also provide their own unique math problems.

We hope you and your child will enjoy the challenges and games in this book in the same way you enjoy playing sports, and that you'll both say:

I LOVE MATH!

The Editors
Time-Life for Children

It's time for the big race! Turn to page 54 to find out who is fastest!

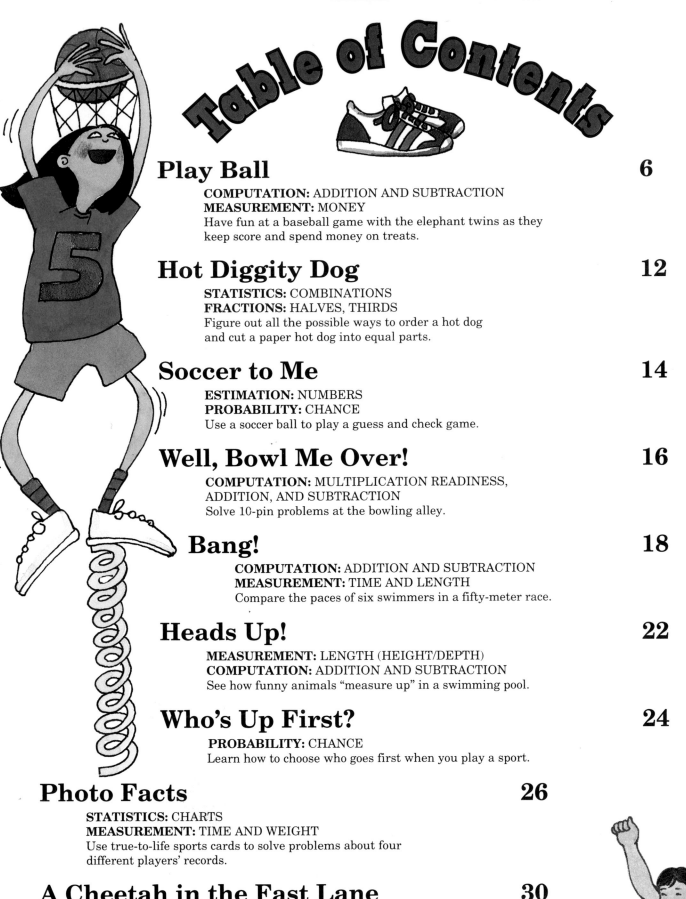

Table of Contents

Used golf balls
10¢ each

PLAY BALL

INNING	1	2	3	4	5	6	7	8	9	TOTAL
RED STRIPES	1	0								
GREEN STRIPES	2	1								

The twins went to see their favorite team play
At Pachyderm Park one hot summer day.

They had each saved $3.00 to spend at the game.
They liked the idea of both having the same.

When they got to their seats they stood for a song.
And Ellen and Hector sang proudly along.

The two kids sat breathless! The Green Stripes
   might win.
They just couldn't wait for the game to begin.

Then Ellen and Hector both spotted a screen,
The biggest TV set that they'd ever seen.

MATH FOCUS: STATISTICS, ADDITION, SUB-TRACTION, AND MONEY. Children use a chart of organized information to solve problems. They also use addition and subtraction to calculate money spent.

Explain to your child that a baseball game is made up of nine innings and that each inning has a "top half" when one team is at bat and a "bottom half" when the other team is at bat. RBI means "runs batted in."

The screen showed the scoreboard, and one great
    big picture
Of Fred "Hip" O' Potamus, the Green Stripes star
    pitcher.

"How do they score?" "Dad, explain RBI."
"How do they figure the stats for each guy?"

The questions they asked left their father's head
    spinning.
By the time he had answered, it was the third
    inning.

Then somebody shouted, "Let's hear some chatter!"
Ellen and Hector cried, "Swing batter! Swing batter!"

*How many runs do the Red Stripes
have so far?
How about the Green Stripes?
Which team is at bat?*

MORE FUN. On page 9, ask your child what he
or she would buy at the ball game and then have
your child add up the cost of his or her purchases.

The shouting was over, half the inning had ended.
Their attention then shifted to food being vended.

"Peanuts!" "Popcorn!" "Hot dogs with mustard!"
"Ice-cold fruit slushes!" "Coconut custard!"

Ellen and Hector each took out $1.00.
Excited and hungry, they started to holler.

"We'll have the peanuts!" they yelled to the vendor.
$1.00 apiece was what the twins sent her.

8

From person to person their money was passed,
An ancient tradition from games long since past.

From a $1.00 bill, each got a coin back,
And a bag full of peanuts to eat as a snack.

They gobbled their peanuts, then wiped off
        their faces
As one of the players was running the bases.

Then, just as a batter popped the ball up high,
Ellen and Hector saw more stuff to buy.

She bought a pennant. He bought a cap.
Then she counted the money left in her lap.

How much did Ellen spend in all?
How much does she have left from her $3.00?

INNING	1	2	3	4	5	6	7
RED STRIPES	1	0	2	2	0	1	1
GREEN STRIPES	2	1	1	0	0	4	1

Hector snagged a fly ball that he
reached out to fetch.
Then everyone stood for the seventh-
inning stretch.

10

In the top of the eighth, the crowd really roared
When a double was hit and the Red Stripes
    team scored!

At the bottom of the the ninth it was tied 10 to 10,
And everyone wondered which team would win.

The batter was up. The bases were loaded.
He hit a home run and the crowd just exploded!

A grand-slam home run! The scoreboard went wild.
Dad shouted, "Hooray!" The twins danced in the
    aisle.

"Hooray!" yelled the twins. "The Green Stripes
    have won!
Thanks for taking us, Dad! We had lots of fun."

What was the best inning for the Red Stripes?
What was the best inning for the Green Stripes?
The Green Stripes scored 4 runs in the ninth
inning. What was the final score?

HOT Diggity DOG

Look at this scrumptious hot dog! How would you split it so Ellen and Hector could each have the same amount? Cut a paper hot dog into 2 equal parts. How did you do it? How could a hot dog be split evenly with their dad?

These fans are really hungry! How many hot dogs would they have to buy so each of them could have half a hot dog? How much money would they need?

MATH FOCUS: FRACTIONS AND STATISTICS. By dividing paper hot dogs into equal parts, children get hands-on experience with fractions. Children also practice problem-solving skills as they list all the possible topping combinations.

Provide paper and crayons so your child can draw the hot dogs and toppings that he or she creates.

Each of these campers wants a hot dog. So does the counselor. Does the vendor have enough hot dogs on his tray for everyone?

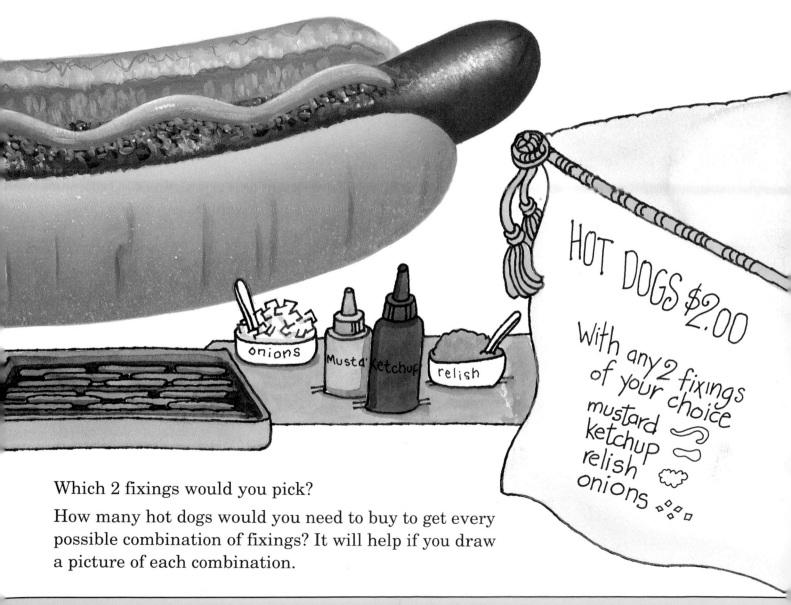

HOT DOGS $2.00

With any 2 fixings of your choice
mustard
ketchup
relish
onions

Which 2 fixings would you pick?

How many hot dogs would you need to buy to get every possible combination of fixings? It will help if you draw a picture of each combination.

MORE FUN. Have your child figure out how many hot dogs you would need in order to give each person in your family half a hot dog.

13

SOCCER to Me

TAKE A GUESS

If you close your eyes and place your finger on this soccer ball 6 times, how many times do you think you'll touch black? How many times do you think you'll touch white? Why do you think so?

FIND OUT

Make a chart like this one. Before each try, guess which color you will touch. Record your guess. After each try, put a mark in the box to show which color you actually touched. How many times did you touch black? How many times did you touch white? How good were your guesses?

MATH FOCUS: ESTIMATION, STATISTICS, AND PROBABILITY. By keeping a record of the number of times a black or a white area of a soccer ball is touched, children explore the probability of a certain thing happening.

14

Have available a pencil and paper. Help your child copy the chart. Before each try, have your child predict which color he or she will probably touch. White will probably be touched more because the ball has more white areas than black.

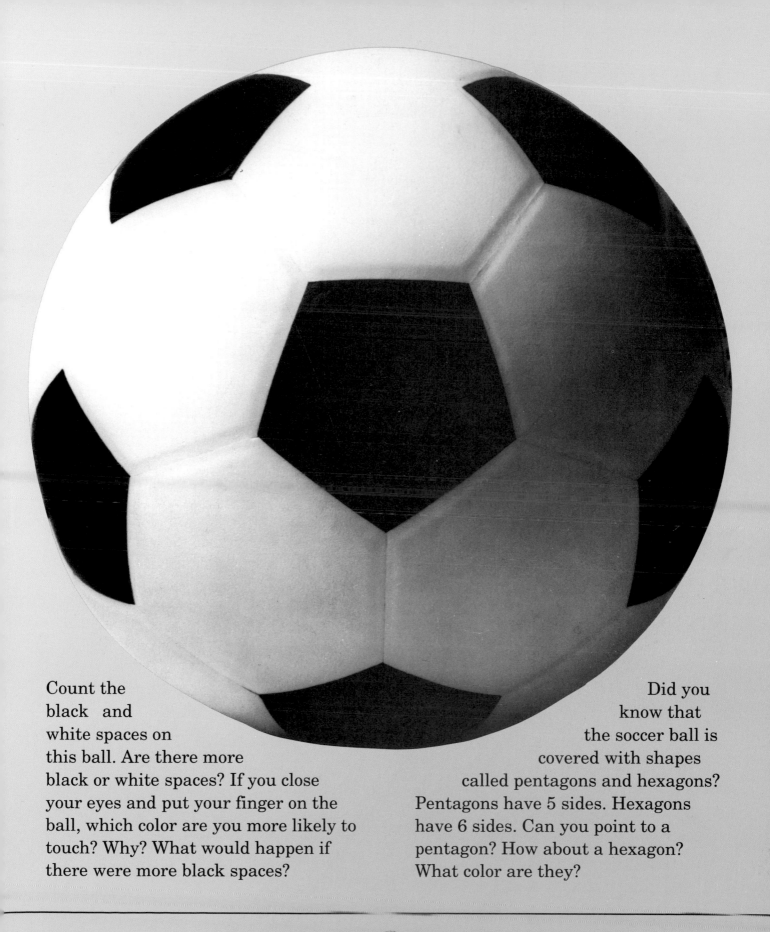

Count the black and white spaces on this ball. Are there more black or white spaces? If you close your eyes and put your finger on the ball, which color are you more likely to touch? Why? What would happen if there were more black spaces?

Did you know that the soccer ball is covered with shapes called pentagons and hexagons? Pentagons have 5 sides. Hexagons have 6 sides. Can you point to a pentagon? How about a hexagon? What color are they?

MORE FUN. Your child can toss a soccer ball back and forth with a friend. Each person can keep track of how many times his or her right thumb touches black, predicting the outcome before he or she tosses the ball each time.

WELL BOWL
me over!

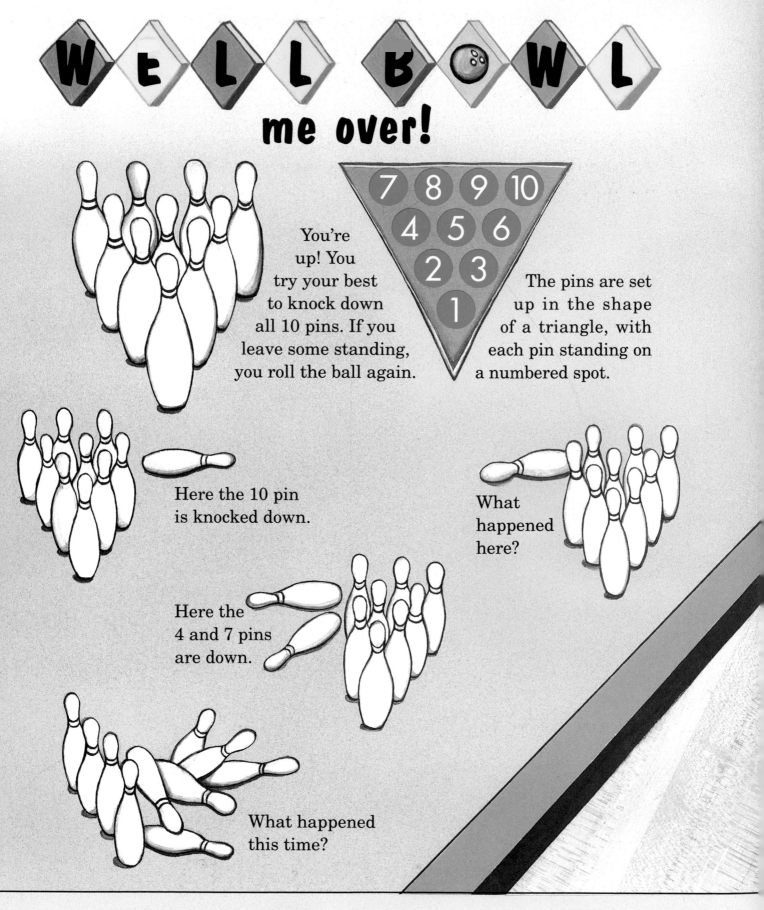

You're up! You try your best to knock down all 10 pins. If you leave some standing, you roll the ball again.

7 8 9 10
4 5 6
2 3
1

The pins are set up in the shape of a triangle, with each pin standing on a numbered spot.

Here the 10 pin is knocked down.

What happened here?

Here the 4 and 7 pins are down.

What happened this time?

Your child can cover numbered pins with cereal pieces to indicate that they have been "knocked down."

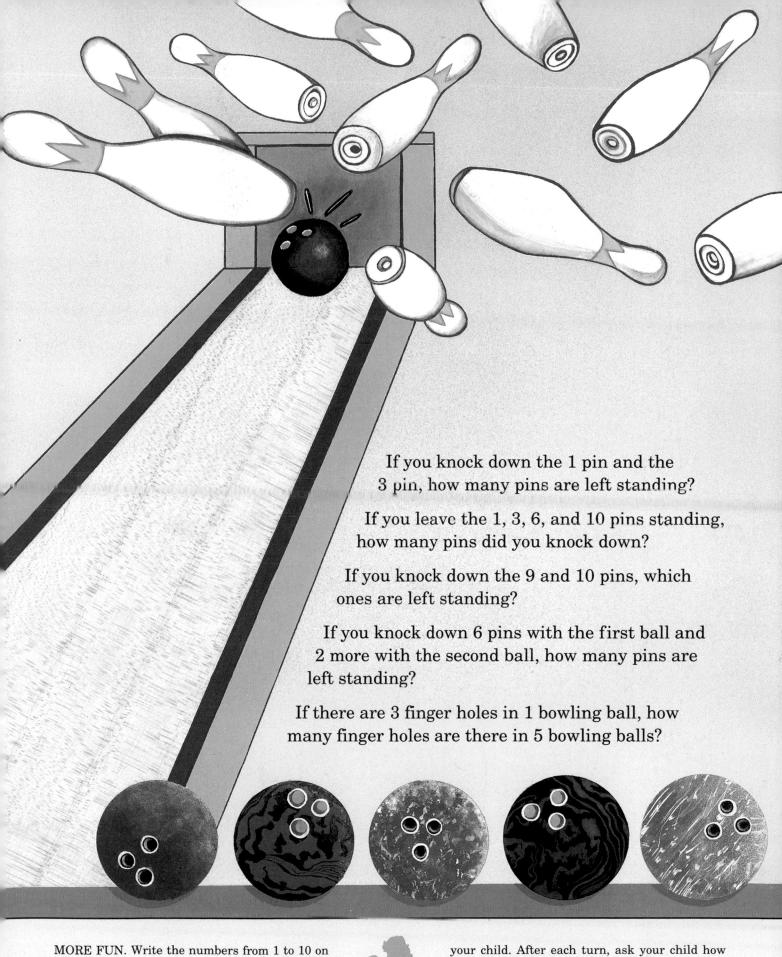

If you knock down the 1 pin and the 3 pin, how many pins are left standing?

If you leave the 1, 3, 6, and 10 pins standing, how many pins did you knock down?

If you knock down the 9 and 10 pins, which ones are left standing?

If you knock down 6 pins with the first ball and 2 more with the second ball, how many pins are left standing?

If there are 3 finger holes in 1 bowling ball, how many finger holes are there in 5 bowling balls?

MORE FUN. Write the numbers from 1 to 10 on ten paper cups and arrange them like bowling pins. Using a small ball, take turns bowling with your child. After each turn, ask your child how many pins were knocked down, and how many remain standing.

BANG!

The starting gun cracks! The three swimmers on the red team and the three on the blue team are in the water in a flash. They'll swim the whole length of the 25-meter pool and the whole length back again.

How many meters long is the race?

Look at Swimmer 4! She's in the lead so far! How many meters has Swimmer 6 swum? Which one is swimming faster?

How many more meters must Swimmer 3 swim before she reaches the wall?

MATH FOCUS: ADDITION, SUBTRACTION, TIME, AND LENGTH. Children use a picture of a swimming pool to solve problems involving addition and subtraction.

Tell your child that the balls on the ropes between the pool lanes in the story are 1 meter apart. Help your child point out the pattern of 4 small white balls and 1 large yellow ball. Have him or her use the yellow balls to count by 5's.

18

The clock lets people know how many seconds have passed since the race began.

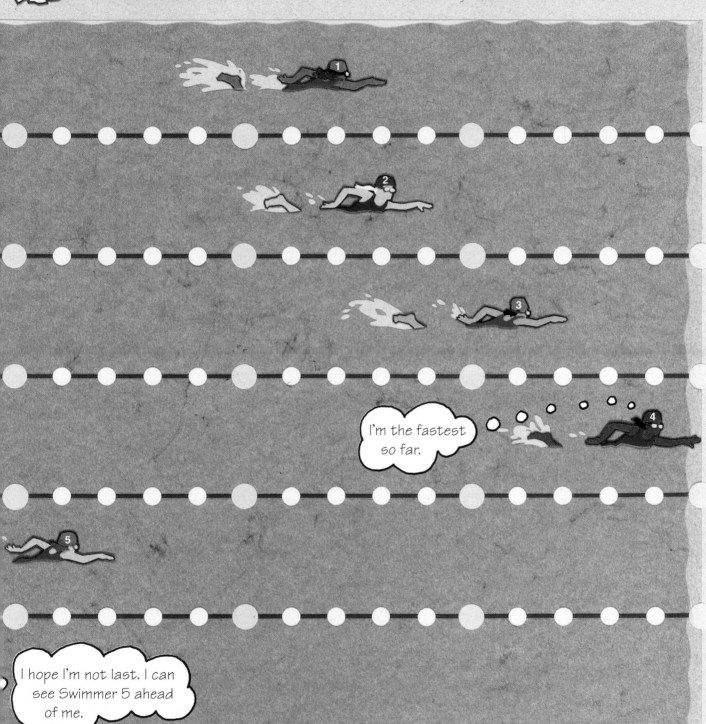

Now all the swimmers have made the turn and started the second half of the race, except for one. Can you find her? Which lane is she in?

Can you find the two swimmers in lanes 3 and 4? Which girl is out in front now? It looks like Swimmer 4 has lost her lead to Swimmer 3!

Swimmer 1 is ahead of which other swimmers? How much farther does she have to swim to reach the end of the race?

The winner just touched the wall! Which swimmer is she? How long did it take her to win the race? Who do you think will come in second and third?

HEADS UP!

It was a hot summer day. "Let's go to the new glass pool in the park," Giraffe said to her friends. So Dog, Pig, Goat, Zebra, and Giraffe all put on their favorite bathing suits. "Don't go in over your head," warned their mothers.

When the five friends got to the pool, they saw signs on the glass edge: 8 feet, 6 feet, 4 feet, 2 feet, 1 foot.

"That's how deep the water is," said Zebra.

"Wow! I can go all the way out to here," said Giraffe at the 8-foot mark. "I'm taller than 8 feet so my head will still be above the water."

8 feet

6 feet

4 feet

Point to the shallow end of the pool. How many feet deep is it? How about the deep end?

If Giraffe stood in the shallow end, would her tail get wet?

MATH FOCUS: LENGTH (HEIGHT/DEPTH), ADDITION, AND SUBTRACTION. Children learn the relative heights of different animals while solving problems involving addition and subtraction.

Have your child guess his or her height and then use a ruler or a yardstick to check. Help your child figure out where he or she could stand safely in the pool by asking questions such as, "Are you between 2 feet tall and 3 feet tall?"

Goat wasn't sure just how tall she was. "How deep can I go?" she asked.

"Start in the shallow water and walk out to deeper water one level at a time. Stop when the water is just under your chin," suggested Pig. So Goat hopped into the shallow end and walked until only her head was above water.

Next, Pig went in to where his little snout was just above the water.

Dog stood at the edge of the pool for a long time. Then he jumped in and dog-paddled in the shallowest part of the pool.

2 feet

1 foot

Which animal is standing in water 5 feet deeper than the shallow end? How deep is it there?

How much deeper than the shallow end is the deep end of the pool?

How tall are you?

Where could you stand with your head above water?

MORE FUN. Have your child guess where the bear and the flamingo might go safely in the pool and then use string or a ruler to check.

23

WHO'S UP FIRST?

Here are some fun ways to help you choose who goes first when you are playing a sport or game.

TOSSING THE BAT

Two players, one from each team, stand facing each other. One of them tosses the bat, handle up, to the other player, who must catch it around the handle with one hand. Then both players take turns putting a hand around the handle just above the other player's hand until one player's hand wraps around the end of the bat. That player decides whether his or her team will be at bat or in the field first. What would you decide? Get a bat or a wrapping paper tube and try this with a partner.

How many hands are on the bat? Who goes first here, the player on the left or the player on the right?

MATH FOCUS: PROBABILITY. Children practice mathematical skills while solving problems about how to choose who goes first when playing a sport or a game.

Have a coin and a baseball bat available and act out each method with your child. Have a family member or a friend help with the last method.

FLIPPING A COIN

Coins have two sides. One side is called the head. The other side is the tail. Here are the heads and tails of our coins.

One player flips a coin in the air and a player from the opposite team calls "heads" or "tails."

The person who flips the coin catches it with one hand and quickly slaps the coin onto the back of the other hand. It looks like this:

HEADS

TAILS

Who makes the decision here?

ONE POTATO, TWO POTATO

Two players, one from each team, face each other. They hold out both arms and make fists. A third person taps each of the players' fists as he or she says each line in this rhyme:

ONE POTATO,
TWO POTATO,
THREE POTATO,
FOUR!

FIVE POTATO,
SIX POTATO,
SEVEN POTATO,
MORE!

The fist tapped on the word "more" must be put behind that player's back. This continues until only one person's fist is still held out. That person decides whether or not his or her team will go first.

Who will decide here?

MORE FUN. Your child can toss a coin 10 times. Before he or she tosses the coin, have him or her predict how many times it will land "heads up." Then have your child try it and see how close he or she comes to the prediction.

PHOTO
FACTS

BASEBALL

SLUGGERS

PAUL

SLUGGERS

PAUL   **OUTFIELD**

Height: 3 ft. 11 in.   **Weight:** 49 lbs.
Bats: Right   **Throws:** Right
Age: 7   **Home:**
                                Allentown, PA

Record

Game	Innings Played	Times at Bat	Hits
1	6	3	2
2	3	2	2
3	7	4	3
4	4	3	1
5	6	3	2

Does Paul weigh more than 50 pounds?

In which game did he play the fewest innings?

How many innings did he play in Game 5?

In which game did he have the fewest times at bat?

In which games did he have the same number of hits?

In which game did he have the most hits?

How many hits did he have in Game 4?

How many times did he bat in both Games 1 and 2?

How many hits did he have in all?

MATH FOCUS: STATISTICS, TIME, WEIGHT, ADDITION, AND SUBTRACTION. Children solve problems by looking at lists of data, selecting what is needed, and adding and subtracting to find the answers.

You can put a ruler or a piece of paper under each row of data to help your child find information in an organized way.

26

KICKERS

KATE		HALFBACK

Height: 4 ft.
Age: 7

Weight: 46 lbs.
Home:
Portland, OR

Record			
Game	Quarters Played	Shots on Goal	Goals
1	2	3	2
2	3	3	2
3	2	1	1
4	3	4	3

How old is Kate?

How much does she weigh?

In how many games did she play for two quarters?

In which games did she play for more than half the game?

In which game did she make the most shots on goal?

In which game did she score the fewest goals?

In which game did she score a goal each time she had a shot on goal?

How many goals did she score in all?

What was the highest number of goals she scored in one game?

MORE FUN. Your child can make his or her own card for a favorite sport. Help him or her write down the information; then your child can attach a recent photo to the front of the card.

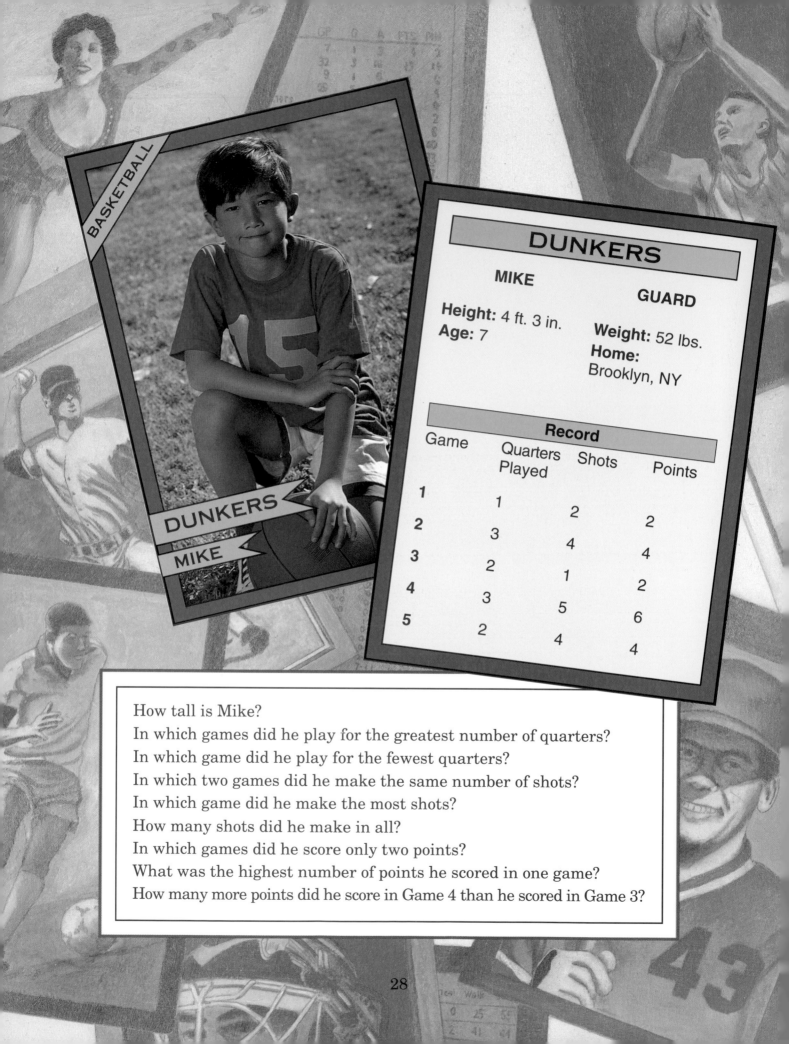

BASKETBALL

DUNKERS
MIKE

DUNKERS

MIKE **GUARD**

Height: 4 ft. 3 in.
Age: 7 **Weight:** 52 lbs.
Home:
Brooklyn, NY

Record			
Game	Quarters Played	Shots	Points
1	1	2	2
2	3	4	4
3	2	1	2
4	3	5	6
5	2	4	4

How tall is Mike?

In which games did he play for the greatest number of quarters?

In which game did he play for the fewest quarters?

In which two games did he make the same number of shots?

In which game did he make the most shots?

How many shots did he make in all?

In which games did he score only two points?

What was the highest number of points he scored in one game?

How many more points did he score in Game 4 than he scored in Game 3?

FLICKERS

LINDA   **FORWARD**

Height: 4 ft. 1 in.   **Weight:** 50 lbs.
Age: 7   **Home:**
                             Lansing, MI

Record

Game	Periods Played	Shots on Goal	Goals
1	1	2	1
2	2	4	1
3	3	5	2
4	2	1	0
5	3	3	2

FIELD HOCKEY

FLICKERS

LINDA

In which game did Linda play for the fewest periods?

How many more periods did she play in Game 2 than in Game 1?

In which games did she play for the greatest number of periods?

How many fewer shots did she make in Game 4 than in Game 5?

In which game did she make the fewest shots?

What was the highest number of shots she made in one game?

In which games did she score the most goals?

How many goals did she score in all?

In which game did she have the fewest shots and the fewest goals?

A Cheetah in the Fast Lane

It was Sports Day at the track. Professor Guesser took a big bag of popcorn and her pompoms and went to watch the fun. She cheered as Ariel Antelope won the long jump. She clapped as KoKo Kangaroo hopped over the high bar. And she whistled as Elmo Elephant threw the shot put farther than anyone else.

Then there was a big commotion. It was time for the cheetahs to race, but they refused to go to the starting line.

"Something's wrong," thought Professor Guesser.

The cheetahs argued with each other and with the referee. Then the referee went to the microphone and announced, "Attention! We have a BIG problem. Is there a problem solver in the house?"

MATH FOCUS: LENGTH. Children compare the distances around the lanes of an oval running track and learn why the starting positions in each one are different.

Have a piece of string available. Help your child measure the distances around the lanes of the track on page 33 and then check your measurements with those shown on pages 34–35.

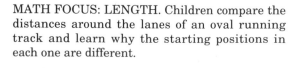

Professor Guesser waved her pompoms. "Maybe I can help!" she replied, and dashed across the field.

"Thank goodness you're here," said the relieved referee.

"What's the problem?" asked Professor Guesser curiously.

"I'm not running another race on this curvy track until this whole thing is straightened out," protested China.

Chi Chi explained, "We've run four practice races today on this track. Each time we race we switch places. But no matter how fast anybody runs, the runner in lane 1, the inside lane, always wins."

Chelsey added, "And whoever runs in lane 4, the outside lane, always loses!"

MORE FUN. Have your child draw a small circle inside a large circle. Then time your child as he or she traces first around the large circle, then around the small circle. Compare the times.

Professor Guesser got out her notebook and sketched a diagram of the track. "Would you be willing to run one practice run so I can observe?"

"Sure," said China. "I'll run in lane 1. You'll see that I'll come in first."

The four cheetahs went to the starting line, and when they were ready, the referee blew his whistle. Professor Guesser watched as the cheetahs sped around the track. She jotted her observations in her notebook.

As China had predicted, she won the race easily. Charo, who ran in the outside lane, lane 4, came across the line last.

"I think I see what's wrong," said Professor Guesser. "Let's test my theory to see if my guess is right."

Professor Guesser placed a huge roll of colored ribbon in each lane. She tied a ribbon to each runner's waist.

"Take the same lanes you ran in before, but this time walk slowly around the track and let your ribbons unwind behind you," she said.

The runners followed Professor Guesser's instructions and walked around the track. China, in lane 1, crossed the finish line first and Charo, in lane 4, crossed the finish line last.

33

Are all the ribbons the same length? Use string to measure around each lane to find out.

Professor Guesser cut each ribbon at the finish line. "Let's see if each cheetah is running the same distance," she said as she and the referee tied the cut ends to a stick. The cheetahs walked forward until each ribbon was straight.

"Look! The ribbons are different lengths," said the referee.

"Just as I suspected!" said the professor. "The runner in lane 1 was running a much shorter distance than the other runners."

"So how do we make the race fair?" asked Chelsey.

"The finish line has to be the same for everyone. We'll have to use one ribbon to measure equal distances in each lane," began Professor Guesser.

"Which ribbon should we measure with?" asked the referee.
"Let's choose the shortest ribbon: the one from lane 1," said Chi Chi.

"Fine," said the professor. "Put one end of the shortest ribbon on the finish line in lane 4. Stretch out the ribbon along the lane so it's flat. Put the starting line for lane 4 at the other end of the ribbon. Do the same for lanes 3, 2, and 1. Then all of the running distances will be the same and the race will be fair."

Are the starting lines in the right places?

Use a piece of string to make sure the distances around each lane are the same.

"Thank you," said Chi Chi. "Now we can run the race!"

"This time it won't matter which lane you run in. The race will be fair," said Professor Guesser.

The cheetahs each went to their own starting line. Professor Guesser held her hat high in the air. "One for the money, two for the show, three to get ready, and four to go!" she said as she dropped her hat.

36

Photo finish

The cheetahs ran as hard and as fast as they could. China took the lead, then Charo, then Chelsey. Chi Chi gained on Chelsey. The four cheetahs were neck and neck as they came down the last stretch. A photo finish!

Professor Guesser waited for the photo to develop. "Look," she exclaimed. "It was China by a nose!"

Then the referee announced the next event, the turtle marathon race. "There's no hurry now," laughed the professor, as she and the four cheetahs settled into the stands to watch the turtles take their turn around the track.

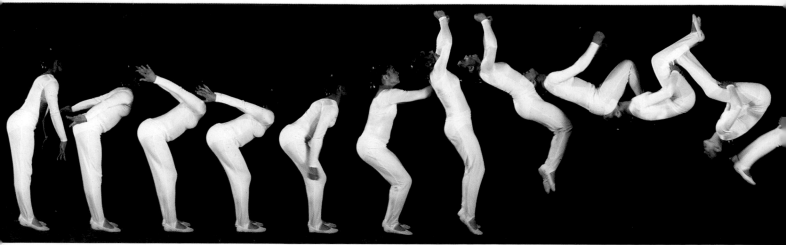

These pictures of a pole-vaulter are all mixed up. Can you tell the correct order?

Which picture shows what happened first?

Which picture shows what happened second? Third? Fourth?

Which picture shows the last thing that happened?

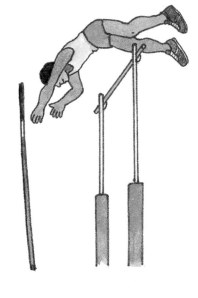

Now tell the order of the pictures of the diver.

Point to the pictures and say, "This happened first. This happened second. This happened third. This happened fourth. This happened last." Tell why you think so.

MATH FOCUS: LOGICAL THINKING AND ORDINAL NUMBERS. By describing the sequence of a picture story, children apply reasoning skills and use positional number words.

Have your child describe what is happening in each pole vault scene. Then have your child tell the order of each picture and his or her reasoning for deciding on that order. Follow the same procedure for the diving scenes.

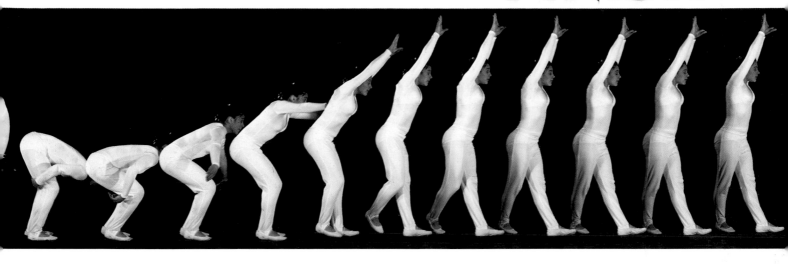

MORE FUN. Your child can choose a favorite sport and draw five simple scenes depicting that sport. Then he or she can cut out the scenes, arrange them in nonsequential order, and challenge family members to rearrange them in sequential order.

MATH FOCUS: STATISTICS AND LOGICAL THINKING. By sorting and classifying things with Venn diagrams, children make comparisons, a skill necessary for problem solving.

You and another family member can take the parts of the two cats in the story and read it to your child. If your child can read, he or she can take the part of one of the cats.

Which ball is it?

MORE FUN. Your child can gather different types of footwear (shoes, sandals, boots, slippers) from family members and make up a question involving any two of the following attributes: size, shape, color, or function. Then your child can make circles out of string to sort the footwear and find the answer.

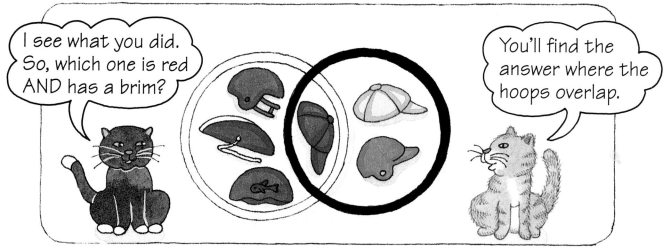

Which one is it?

All About Me

What can you learn about me from my hula hoops?

FIRST NAME **LAST NAME**

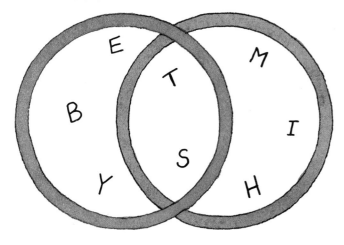

B E T Y S M I H

What are my first and last names?
Which letters do I have in both names?

How many kids are on my team?
Who is both on my team and lives on my street?

KIDS ON MY TEAM **KIDS ON MY STREET**

Joe
Pam
Sue
Bill
Val
Ted
Jean

FRUIT SNACKS **FAVORITE AFTER-GAME SNACKS**

Do I have an after-game snack that's a fruit? What is it?

MORE FUN. Have your child make up some "All About Me" diagrams about himself or herself.

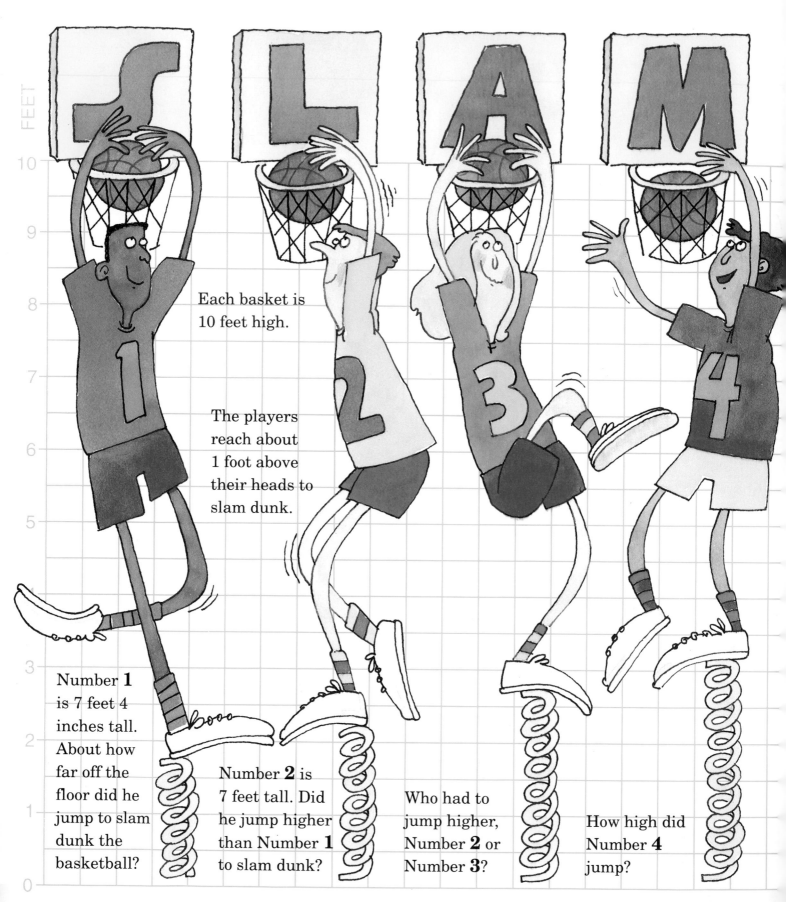

FEET

10

9

8 — Each basket is 10 feet high.

7

6 — The players reach about 1 foot above their heads to slam dunk.

5

4

3

2 — Number **1** is 7 feet 4 inches tall. About how far off the floor did he jump to slam dunk the basketball?

1 — Number **2** is 7 feet tall. Did he jump higher than Number **1** to slam dunk?

Who had to jump higher, Number **2** or Number **3**?

How high did Number **4** jump?

0

MATH FOCUS: LENGTH (HEIGHT) AND STATISTICS. Children use a graph to solve problems while practicing mathematical skills.

44

Help your child figure out that each square represents a height of half a foot. As there are several different ways to find the answers to each question, have your child describe the methods he or she used.

DUNK!

Number **7** is 5 feet 6 inches tall. She barely made it. But who jumped higher than anyone else?

Number **5** is 5 feet 10 inches tall. Compare her jump with Number **2**'s jump.

Number **6** needed to get a good running start so he could slam dunk. Why? About how tall is he?

Why do you think Number **8** did not try to slam dunk? Can he make a basket with this kind of shot?

FEET

10 9 8 7 6 5 4 3 2 1 0

MORE FUN. Use a yardstick to measure how high your child can jump on 3 successive tries.

COUNT ME IN

The Red Hots slid down the morning-glory vines to the kickball diamond. They were ready for the game.

But the Sunshine Squad wasn't ready to play. They were standing in a circle pointing at each other and arguing.

Dotty, the captain of the Red Hots, went to see what was going on. "What's holding you up?" she asked.

"We need 7 players to play kickball. But I only count 6 of us," said Bugsy, the Sunshine Squad's captain. He counted the other team members carefully. "1, 2, 3, 4, 5, 6!"

"If you don't have enough players you'll have to forfeit the game. We will win automatically," teased Dotty.

How many players are on the Sunshine Squad?

MATH FOCUS: COUNTING AND LOGICAL THINKING. By using one-to-one correspondence to count a given number of objects, children deepen their awareness of number skills.

46

Before reading the story have your child explain what he or she thinks the title means; after the story discuss the title again and see if your child's understanding of it has changed.

"We're not going to let you win so easily," said Bea. "I'll check the number another way." She looked carefully at the other members of her team. "I see 3 tall players and 3 short players. And 3 plus 3 equals 6!"

"That couldn't be right!" protested Domino. "I see 2 short players and 4 tall ones."

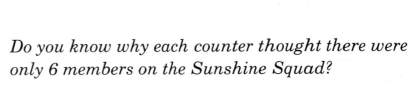

"2 plus 4 is still 6," said Dotty.

"Oh, no! We're going to lose the tournament because we don't have 7 players on our team," cried Domino.

Do you know why each counter thought there were only 6 members on the Sunshine Squad?

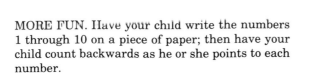

MORE FUN. Have your child write the numbers 1 through 10 on a piece of paper; then have your child count backwards as he or she points to each number.

"I can't let this go on!" shouted the umpire. "There are 7 players on your team!"

"Every time we counted ourselves we counted 6 players. How can there be 7 players?" asked Bea.

"Let me count you," said the umpire. "Bugsy is 1, Bea is 2, Domino is 3, Dewy is 4, Mark is 5, Ringo is 6, and Elli is 7!"

The Sunshine Squad was astounded. "You're a magician!" gasped Bugsy.

"Not really. He just has good math skills," winked Dotty. "I think I understand what you did. When you counted, each of you made the same mistake. You forgot to count yourself."

"Right!" shouted the umpire. "**PLAY BALL**!"

Count On Us

Have fun with the Red Hots.

Find the ladybug with the same number of dots as days in a week.

Find the ladybug with half a dozen dots.

Find the ladybug with the greatest number of dots.

Find the ladybug with the fewest number of dots.

Point to the ladybug whose dots equal the number of sides on a square.

Which ladybugs have an even number of dots?

Which ladybugs have an odd number of dots?

DOTTY

FRED

IRIS

PETE

JANE

PAUL

JACK

MATH FOCUS: COUNTING AND NUMBER PATTERNS. Children use problem-solving strategies to count dots and identify patterns on ladybugs.

As your child finds each ladybug on page 50 have him or her say how many dots it has. To help your child solve each problem on page 51 have him or her first tell how many dots are on the ladybugs in each row, for example: "2, 4, blank, 8, 10."

MORE FUN. Your child can make up a different set of questions for the ladybugs on page 50 and challenge family members to solve them.

ANSWERS, PAGE 51. Top row: 6 dots; middle row: 4 dots, 6 dots; bottom row: 9 dots.

MATH FOCUS: ADDITION AND SUBTRAC-TION. By adding 2, 3, 4, or 5 numbers together, children explore mental arithmetic.

Encourage your child to solve each puzzle "in his or her head." Have your child think out loud and explain his or her strategy for finding the answer.

I scored 16 points with 2 arrows. Each arrow landed on a different number. Where did the arrows land?

I scored 16 points with 2 arrows. Both arrows landed on the same number. Where did the arrows land?

I scored 8 points with 3 arrows. 2 of the arrows landed on the same number. Where did the arrows land?

I scored 14 points with 2 arrows. Tell one way the arrows could have landed. Tell another way.

MORE FUN. Help your child make up a few puzzles like the ones on these pages. Have family members try to solve them.

AMAZING ANIMAL ATHLETES

When you walk, you go at a speed of about 4 miles an hour. That means if you walked for 1 hour without stopping, you would walk a distance of about 4 miles.

How fast can you run? The speediest humans can run at a speed of more than 20 miles an hour!

Animals swim, run, and fly at a wide variety of speeds.

How do you think you'd do in a race with a giraffe, a snake, a sailfish, a dragonfly, a cheetah, a lion, and a swift? Take a look at the bar graph on the next page to find out.

MATH FOCUS: GRAPHS, TIME, AND LENGTH (HEIGHT). Children read a graph and compare information to solve problems.

Help your child figure out the speed of each animal shown on the graph. Point out that the speed of the snake, for example, is just a bit less than 10 miles an hour, so it's probably 8 miles an hour.

SPEEDS OF RACERS

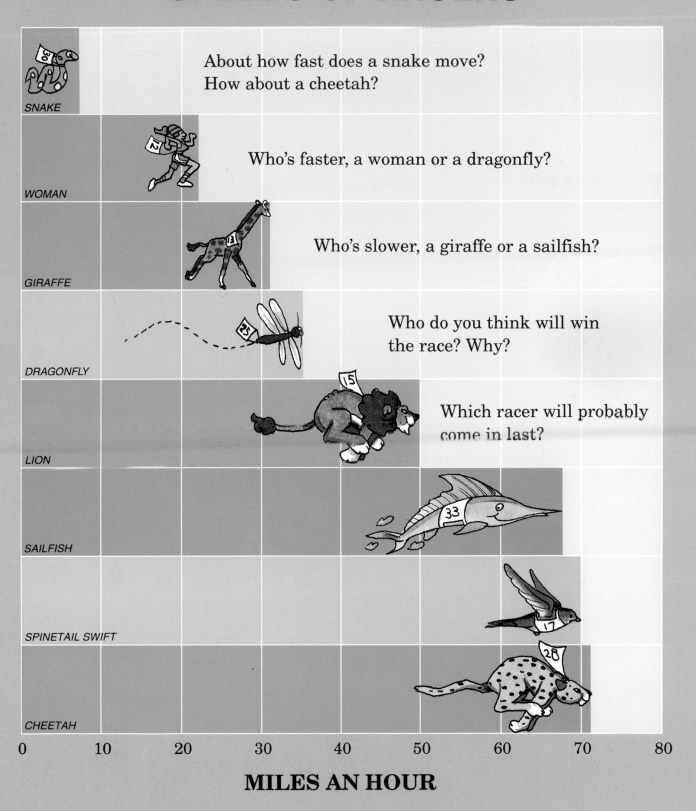

RACERS

SNAKE

About how fast does a snake move?
How about a cheetah?

WOMAN

Who's faster, a woman or a dragonfly?

GIRAFFE

Who's slower, a giraffe or a sailfish?

DRAGONFLY

Who do you think will win
the race? Why?

LION

Which racer will probably
come in last?

SAILFISH

SPINETAIL SWIFT

CHEETAH

0   10   20   30   40   50   60   70   80

MILES AN HOUR

MORE FUN. Your child can make up more questions about the speeds of the animals shown on the graph or about the speeds of the racers on pages 56 and 57.

Who would win this race?
How many seconds after the cheetah would the man cross
the finish line?
Who would probably win the 200-yard dash?

Who would probably win this standing long-jump contest?
How much farther than the woman can the frog jump?

56

How much longer than the fish does it take the woman to swim 100 yards?

Does it take the woman more than a minute or less than a minute to swim 100 yards?

Would the kangaroo be able to jump over a bar that is 8 feet high?

Would the man be able to jump over that bar?

YOU TRY IT!

Try each of these events.
Keep a record of how you do in each one.

EVENT 1

BASKETBALL
Get a small ball. Make a throw line 1 foot from an empty wastebasket. Guess how many times you can get the ball in the basket in 5 throws. Stand just behind the throw line, aim, and shoot. Keep moving your throw line farther away by 1 foot until you miss the basket all 5 throws. How many "baskets" did you make at each distance? How good was your guess?

EVENT 2

THE STANDING BROAD JUMP
Stand on a starting line. Guess how many inches you can jump. Take a deep breath and jump as far as you can. Measure the distance from the starting line to the spot where your heels touched the ground. Do the broad jump again. Which jump was longer? Was your guess close?

EVENT 3

THE RUNNING JUMP
Make a starting line. Guess how many inches you can jump if you run up to the line and jump. Try it. Measure the distance you jumped. Do another running jump. Which jump was longer? How good was your guess?

MATH FOCUS: ESTIMATION, TIME, AND LENGTH. In these home sports events, children get direct experience in guessing how they will perform and then checking their estimates.

Have available a stopwatch or a watch with a second hand, a ruler or yardstick, a wastebasket, a small ball, milk containers or shoeboxes, string, and a large rubber ball.

EVENT 4

THE HURDLES
Place 7 empty milk containers about 3 feet from each other. About how many seconds do you think it will take you to jump over the hurdles? Try it. Have someone time you. If you knock down a hurdle, add 2 seconds to your race time. How close was your guess? Jump the hurdles again. Compare your time for the second race to the time for your first race.

EVENT 5

THE BALANCE BEAM
Put a long piece of string on the ground. This is your balance beam. About how many seconds do you think it will take you to walk the beam? Try it. Walk with your head up. Don't look at your feet. If you step off the string, start again. Have someone time you. How good was your guess?

EVENT 6

BALL BOUNCING
How many times do you think you can bounce a ball in 30 seconds? Have someone time you and count the bounces. How close was your guess? Bounce the ball for 1 minute. Compare the number of bounces in 1 minute to the number of bounces in 30 seconds.

MORE FUN. Help your child plan a "field day" with friends using these homemade sports events.

SPORTS Riddles

WHO'S WHO?

Mary and Sue are in Field Day events at school. One girl is in the long jump event, and the other girl is in the shot put event. The girl with the 3-letter name does not jump. Who does what?

THE PROBLEM IS NICKELS.

Andy bought a hot dog for $1.25. He paid for it with a dollar bill and 4 coins. He did not get any change. How many of the coins were nickels?

MATH FOCUS: LOGICAL THINKING, GEOMETRY, TIME, AND MONEY. By solving riddles involving different areas of mathematics, children learn to analyze information and to apply reasoning skills.

Have available a dollar bill, 4 quarters, 4 dimes, 4 nickels, and 4 pennies.

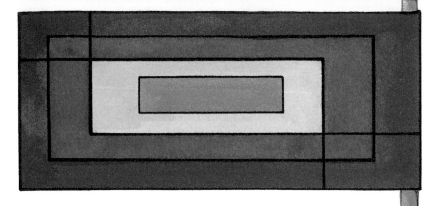

IT'S A PUZZLE!

How many rectangles can you find in the school flag?

WHAT'S HIS NUMBER?

The number on the back of John's shirt is greater than 30. It is less than 40. It is not an even number. If you switch the digits, you will get the same number. What is John's number?

PICK A NUMBER.

1   4   10

Amy is in fifth grade. She is

☐ years old and is a runner.

She exercises for ☐ hour

each day. She starts at 3 o'clock

and finishes at ☐ o'clock.

MORE FUN. Your child can draw a geometric picture and then challenge family members to find all the shapes hidden in it.

ANSWERS. Sue is in the shot put, Mary is in the long jump; 3 nickels; 12 rectangles; John's number is 33; Amy is 10, exercises for 1 hour, and finishes at 4 o'clock.

Caldonia and the Calculator

Caldonia lives on the edge of the Goofy Golfers' Golf Club. As well as being a bit prickly she is a sharp animal. Caldonia decides to collect lost golf balls. As she finds them she puts them into her calculator wagon. Then she uses the calculator to figure out how many balls she has at the end of each day. Use your calculator to help Caldonia keep track of how many balls she has collected by the end of the week.

On Monday Caldonia finds 26 golf balls.

On Tuesday Caldonia finds 8 balls. How many golf balls does she have now? Did you add or subtract?

On Wednesday Caldonia sees her friend Tilly the Turtle take 11 golf balls out of the calculator wagon. Tilly is a bit nearsighted and thinks they are turtle eggs. How many golf balls does Caldonia have in the calculator wagon now? Did you use the + key or the − key?

On Thursday Caldonia finds 10 golf balls. What is the total number of golf balls Caldonia has now? Did you use the sign for addition or the sign for subtraction?

On Friday Caldonia's wagon tips over and 11 balls roll into the pond. How many does she have now? How did you find the answer?

On Saturday evening, after the busiest day at the golf course, Caldonia finds 30 golf balls! How many does she have now? How did you find out?

On Sunday Caldonia puts up a sign. She sells 9 golf balls. How much money does she get? How many golf balls are left in her wagon?

Used golf balls 10¢ each

TIME-LIFE for CHILDREN®

Publisher: Robert H. Smith
Associate Publisher and Managing Editor: Neil Kagan
Assistant Managing Editor: Patricia Daniels
Editorial Directors: Jean Burke Crawford, Allan Fallow,
   Karin Kinney, Sara Mark, Elizabeth Ward
Director of Marketing: Margaret Mooney
Product Managers: Cassandra Ford,
   Shelley L. Schimkus
Director of Finance: Lisa Peterson
Financial Analyst: Patricia Vanderslice
Administrative Assistant: Barbara A. Jones
Production Manager: Prudence G. Harris
Production: Celia Beattie
Supervisor of Quality Control: James King

Produced by Kirchoff/Wohlberg, Inc.
866 United Nations Plaza
New York, New York 10017

Series Director: Mary Jane Martin
Creative Director: Morris A. Kirchoff
Mathematics Director: Jo Dennis
Designer: Jessica A. Kirchoff
Assistant Designers: Brian Collins, Daniel Moreton,
   Judith Schwartz
Contributing Writers: Gloria Armstrong,
   Anne M. Miranda, Shereen Rutman
Managing Editor: Nancy Pernick
Editors: Susan M. Darwin, Beth Grout, David McCoy

Cover Illustration: Joe Veno

Illustration Credits: Liz Callen, pp. 6–13, pp. 44–45; Steve
Cieslawski, pp. 26–29; Jessica A. Kirchoff, front end papers;
Tom Leonard, pp. 6–13, pp. 46–51; Susan Lexa, pp. 38–39;
Don Madden, pp. 30–37; Jane McCreary, pp. 60–61; Frank
McShane, pp. 18–21; Daniel Moreton, back end papers;
Diane Paterson, pp. 14–15; Andy San Diego, pp. 62–63;
Judith Schwartz, pp. 16–17; Joe Veno, pp. 22–25, pp. 54–59;
Alexandra Wallner, pp. 40–43, pp. 52–53

First printing. Printed in U.S.A.
Published simultaneously in Canada.

Time Life Inc. is a wholly owned subsidiary of THE TIME INC.
BOOK COMPANY.

TIME-LIFE is a trademark of Time Warner Inc. U.S.A.

For subscription information, call 1-800-621-7026.

CONSULTANTS

Mary Jane Martin spent 17 years working in elementary school classrooms as a teacher and reading consultant; for seven of those years she was a first-grade teacher. The second half of her career has been devoted to publishing. During this time she has helped create and produce a wide variety of innovative elementary programs, including two mathematics textbook series.

Jo Dennis has worked as a teacher and math consultant in England, Australia, and the United States for more than 20 years. Most recently, she has helped develop and write several mathematics textbooks for kindergarten, first grade, and second grade.

Catherine Motz Peterson is a curriculum specialist who spent five years developing an early elementary mathematics program for the nationally acclaimed Fairfax County Public Schools in Virginia. She is also mathematics consultant to the University Of Maryland, Catholic University, and the Fredrick County Public Schools in Maryland. Ms. Peterson is the director of the Capitol Hill Day School in Washington, D.C.

Dr. Helene Joy Silverman is a professor of early childhood and elementary education at Herbert H. Lehman College, City University of New York, and a co-director of the New York City Mathematics Project. Following service as a teacher in the New York City public schools, she became an author of children's materials, a contributor to several math textbook series, and a math consultant to many school districts.

Judy Heard is an elementary school teacher in the public school system of Fairfax County, Virginia. She was a first-grade teacher for almost 14 years, and currently teaches math in grades 1 through 6. In 1990, she was awarded the Virginia Elementary Math Teacher Award by the Virginia Council of Teachers of Mathematics. In 1991, the National Science Foundation presented her with the Presidential Award for Excellence in Teaching Elementary Mathematics, an award given each year to one teacher from every state.

Photography Credits: pp. 14–15, Justin Kirchoff; pp. 24–25, American
Numismatic Society, NY; pp. 26–27, John C. Pittman Photography;
pp. 28–29, Ken Lax; pp. 38–39, Globus Brothers, The Stock Market.

Library of Congress Cataloging-in-Publication Data
Play ball: sports math.
　　　　　　p.　　cm. —— (I love math)
　　　　Summary: Uses stories, poems, riddles, games, and hands-
on activities, all related to various sports, to teach early math skills.
　　　　ISBN 0-8094-9970-3
　　　　1. Mathematics—Study and teaching (Elementary)—
Juvenile literature. 2. Sports—Juvenile literature. [1. Mathematics.
2. Mathematical recreations. 3. Sports—Miscellanea.] I. Time-Life for
Children (Firm) II. Series.
QA135.5.P57　　1993
372.7—dc20　　　　　　　　　　　　92-38622
　　　　　　　　　　　　　　　　　　　　CIP
　　　　　　　　　　　　　　　　　　　　AC

ickball on a Roll

The Number of Players: 2

The Object of the Game: To have more runs at the end of the game.

The Playing Pieces: A pair of dice; 4 identical markers for each player, such as 4 dimes and 4 nickels; and pencil and paper to tally total numbers of runs and outs for each player.

The Play:

- Players take turns being the kicker and the pitcher. On each turn, both players roll 1 die.

- The kicker goes first. If the pitcher rolls a greater number than the kicker rolls, the kicker is out. After 3 outs, the kicker and pitcher change positions.

- If the kicker rolls a greater number than the pitcher, the lesser number is subtracted from the greater number, and the kicker moves a marker that number of bases. Play continues with the kicker using a new marker for each roll, moving any markers already on base ahead as needed to free a base for the new marker.

- If both players roll the same number, the kicker "walks" by moving the new marker 1 base.

- HOME RUN: When the kicker wins the roll with a 4 or 5 the marker advances around all 4 bases, bringing in all other markers on base.

The Winner: After each player has been the kicker twice, the player with the higher score wins.

Math Concepts: Number recognition. Number comparisons. Subtraction facts to 6.